I0820956

NORTH AMERICAN FIELD GUIDES

SPIDERS

Samantha S. Bell

Field Guides

An Imprint of Abdo Reference | abdobooks.com

CONTENTS

What Are Spiders? **4**
How to Use This Book **6**

Cellar Spiders
Daddy Longlegs Spider 8
Northwestern Cellar Spider 9

Cobweb Spiders
Brown Widow 10
Common House Spider 11
False Black Widow 12
Northern Black Widow 13
Red Widow 14
Southern Black Widow 15
Triangulate Cobweb Spider 16
Western Black Widow 17

Crab Spiders
American Green Crab Spider 18
Bark Crab Spider 19
Elegant Crab Spider 20
Goldenrod Crab Spider 21
Northern Crab Spider 22
Swift Crab Spider 23
Tuberculated Crab Spider 24
Whitebanded Crab Spider 25

Funnel Weavers
Hobo Spider 26
Pennsylvania Grass Spider 27

Ground Spiders
Parson Spider 28
Variegated Spider 29

Meshweavers
Black Lace Weaver 30
Hacklemesh Weaver 31

Jumping Spiders
Ant-Mimicking Jumping Spider 32
Apache Jumping Spider 33
Bold Jumper 34
Bronze Jumper 35
Canopy Jumping Spider 36
Common Hentz Jumping Spider 37
Dimorphic Jumping Spider 38
Emerald Jumping Spider 39
Gray Wall Jumping Spider 40
Magnolia Green Jumping Spider 41
Regal Jumping Spider 42
Zebra Spider 43

Lynx Spiders
Green Lynx Spider 44
Striped Lynx Spider 45

Nursery Web Spiders
American Nursery Web Spider 46
Dark Fishing Spider 47
Six-Spotted Fishing Spider 48
White-Banded Fishing Spider 49

Orb Weavers
Arabesque Orb Weaver 50
Arrowhead Spider 51
Arrowshaped Micrathena 52
Banded Garden Spider 53
Barn Spider 54
Cat-Faced Spider 55
Cross Orb Weaver 56
Feather-Legged Orb Weaver 57
Golden Silk Orb Weaver 58
Hentz Orb Weaver 59
Humped Trashline Orb Weaver 60
Long-Jawed Orb Weaver 61
Marbled Orb Weaver 62
Orchard Orb Weaver 63

Silver Argiope....64
Spiny-Backed Orb Weaver....65
Toadlike Bolas Spider....66
Yellow Garden Spider....67

Purseweb Spiders

Blue Purseweb Spider....68
Red-Legged Purseweb Spider....69

Recluse Spiders

Brown Recluse....70
Desert Recluse....71

Running Crab Spiders

Broad-Faced Sac Spider....72
Slender Crab Spider....73
Turf Running Spider....74
Yellow Sac Spider....75

Sheet Weavers

Black-Tailed Red Sheetweaver....76
Bowl and Doily Spider....77
Filmy Dome Spider....78
Hammock Spider....79

Tarantulas

Curlyhair Tarantula....80
Desert Blonde Tarantula....81
Desert Tarantula....82
Johnny Cash Tarantula....83
Mexican Pink Tarantula....84
Mexican Red Rump Tarantula....85
Mexican Redknee Tarantula....86
Texas Brown Tarantula....87

Trapdoor Spiders

California Trapdoor Spider....88
Folding-Door Spider....89

Wolf Spiders

Beach Wolf Spider....90
Brush-Legged Wolf Spider....91
Burrowing Wolf Spider....92
Carolina Wolf Spider....93
Dotted Wolf Spider....94
Rabid Wolf Spider....95
Thin-Legged Wolf Spider....96
Tiger Wolf Spider....97

Other Unique Spiders

Common Pirate Spider....98
Garden Ghost Spider....99
Giant Crab Spider....100
Huntsman Spider....101
Ogre-Faced Spider....102
Southeastern Wandering Spider....103
Southern House Spider....104
Spitting Spider....105
Spruce-Fir Moss Spider....106
Woodlouse Spider....107

Glossary....108
To Learn More....109
Photo Credits....110

WHAT ARE SPIDERS?

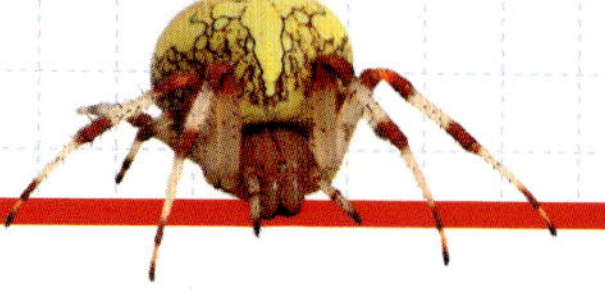

Spiders belong to a group of animals called arachnids. This group also includes mites, ticks, and scorpions. All spiders have eight legs, and their bodies are divided into two sections. These are the cephalothorax in front and the abdomen in back. Most spiders have eight eyes. Some species have only two, four, or six eyes. Some cave-dwelling spiders have no eyes at all. The smallest spider in the world is the Samoan moss spider, which is 0.013 inches (0.033 cm) long. The largest is the Goliath birdeater. It has a leg span of almost 12 inches (30.5 cm).

Every spider species produces silk. The silk comes from special body parts called spinnerets. These are usually located at the rear of the abdomen. The silk is pulled out by gravity or by the spider's hind legs. Many spiders spin the silk into webs to capture food. Some wrap their prey in silk before they eat it. Some use silk to line their burrows. Spiders can also use their silk to make egg cases.

All spiders are carnivorous. This means they feed on other animals. While most eat insects, some spiders also eat frogs, lizards, and fish. Spiders play an important role in controlling insect populations, especially pests such as flies, mosquitoes, and moths. Without spiders, pest insects could ruin crops and other food supplies.

All spiders are venomous. They use their venom to paralyze their prey. However, only a small percentage of spiders are dangerous to humans. They may bite if cornered or trapped.

SPIDER IDENTIFICATION

There are about 4,000 species of spiders in North America. Globally, there are around 50,000 known species of spiders. Scientists believe there are many more types of spiders yet to be discovered.

Scientists often classify spiders according to how they catch their food. Some spiders use webs, while others hunt their prey. Web builders are also grouped by the types of webs they make. Spiders are further classified by their body structure, such as how their eyes are arranged or how many claws they have. Some characteristics can be seen only with a microscope.

While webs help identify spiders, a web is not always present. When identifying spiders, it is helpful to also note the following characteristics:

- Size: The spider's body length. For most species, the male spider is smaller than the female.
- North American Range: Where the spider is found in North America.
- Habitat: The types of places where the spider can be found, such as in forests, deserts, or buildings.
- Diet: The types of food the spider eats.

HOW TO USE THIS BOOK

Tab shows the spider category.

JUMPING SPIDERS

BOLD JUMPER *(PHIDIPPUS AUDAX)*

The spider's common name appears here.

The bold jumper is a black, hairy spider. It has a pattern of
white, yellow, or orange spots on the top of its abdomen.
... over their eyes that look like
...ng spiders, bold jumpers hunt
... watch for prey with their sharp
...ce on it. Bold jumpers quickly jump
away ...ators.

FUN FACT
Bold jumping spiders can leap up to 50 times the length of their bodies. That is a little more than two feet (0.6 m).

Fun Facts give interesting information about spiders.

HOW TO SPOT

Size: 0.23 to 0.6 inches (6 to 15 mm) long

North American Range: Southern Canada, throughout the United States, and northern Mexico

Habitat: Grasslands, prairies, open woodlands, fields, backyards, gardens, and buildings

Diet: Other spiders and insects including boll weevils and moths

How to Spot boxes give information about the spider's size, range, habitat, and diet.

34

BRONZE JUMPER *(ERIS MILITARIS)*

Bronze jumpers are small to medium brown spiders. Each side of the cephalothorax has a white stripe. The a[...] has a white stripe around it. These spiders prefer [...] sunny places. They are often found crawling on b[...] walls. In the fall, bronze jumpers sometimes gathe[...] same place, such as under tree bark. They may sp[...] winter together. They come out in early spring and summer.

The spider's scientific name appears here.

This paragraph gives information about the spider.

HOW TO SPOT

Size: 0.2 to 0.31 inches (5 to 8 mm) long
North American Range: Throughout most of Canada and the United States
Habitat: Sunny areas with trees and low vegetation; human structures
Diet: Small insects

Images show the spider.

SUPER VISION

Jumping spiders have the best eyesight of all spiders. The two main forward-facing eyes see in high-detail color. The next pair sees in black and white. The other eyes have less detailed vision in black and white. When all eight eyes work together, the spider has a nearly 360-degree view. With such sharp eyesight, jumping spiders can stalk and pounce on their prey with precision.

Sidebars provide additional information about the topic.

DADDY LONGLEGS SPIDER

(PHOLCUS PHALANGIOIDES)

Daddy longlegs spiders are harmless, fragile spiders with very long, thin legs. Daddy longlegs usually build large, flat webs. A female lays clusters of 25 to 60 eggs at a time. The mother wraps the eggs in a thin layer of silk. She hangs upside down and holds the egg sac in her jaws until the eggs hatch. She watches over her young for about nine days. Then the spiderlings leave to build their own webs. The spiders live for about three years.

Female carrying eggs

HOW TO SPOT

Size: 0.23 to 0.31 inches (6 to 8 mm) long

North American Range: Throughout North America

Habitat: Basements, warehouses, garages, sheds, caves, and other dark protected areas

Diet: Insects and other spiders found in homes, often much larger than the daddy longlegs

FUN FACT

The body and legs of the daddy longlegs spider are nearly transparent. Because of this, scientists can use a microscope to see blood cells moving through the spider's body.

NORTHWESTERN CELLAR SPIDER *(PSILOCHORUS HESPERUS)*

The northwestern cellar spider has a small body and long, thin legs. It has a round abdomen with a dark pattern. Despite its name, this spider rarely lives indoors. It lives mostly in natural habitats. In hot, dry areas, it lives under large rocks. After mating, the females can produce several egg sacs. Each sac contains about 24 eggs. The female carries the egg sacs in her jaws until the eggs hatch.

FUN FACT

Northwestern cellar spiders occasionally live in cellars. These underground rooms mimic the spiders' natural cool, moist habitats.

HOW TO SPOT

Size: 0.1 to 0.13 inches (2.5 to 3.3 mm) long

North American Range: Southern British Columbia in Canada and northwestern United States

Habitat: In caves, under rocks, and in abandoned mammal burrows

Diet: Insects

BROWN WIDOW

(LATRODECTUS GEOMETRICUS)

Brown widows are native to Africa but came to Florida in the early 1900s. Most are tan with an orange hourglass shape on the underside of their abdomens. However, they can also be gray, dark brown, or almost black. Adult brown widows look very similar to young black widows. Only female brown widows can bite people. The fangs of the males are too small. The bite is painful but rarely dangerous.

HOW TO SPOT

Size: 0.23 to 0.6 inches (6 to 16 mm) long

North American Range: Southern California and southern United States from Texas to Florida

Habitat: Around homes in closets and garages and in empty containers; also around woody plants

Diet: Insects, lizards, snakes, and small mammals

Female

Male

FUN FACT

When threatened, brown widows often play dead. They drop to the ground and tuck in their legs to appear lifeless.

COMMON HOUSE SPIDER

(PARASTEATODA TEPIDARIORUM)

The common house spider is yellowish brown. It has patterns of brown, gray, and white markings. This spider has extra-long front legs. It builds large, tangled webs. Inside homes, these webs can be found in the corners of rooms and windows or under furniture. After mating, males often share the webs with the females. A female can spin up to 15 egg sacs. Each one holds 100 to 400 eggs.

Egg sacs

HOW TO SPOT

Size: 0.15 to 0.23 inches (3.8 to 6 mm) long

North American Range: Southern Canada and across the United States

Habitat: In barns and houses, under bridges and other structures, and under rocks and boards

Diet: Insects such as flies, mosquitoes, and camel crickets and some spiders

FALSE BLACK WIDOW

(STEATODA GROSSA)

The false black widow is a species of false widow spider. False widows are much less venomous than the black widow. Although similar in size to a black widow spider, the false black widow does not have a red hourglass shape on the underside of the abdomen. Most false black widow spiders are brown or black with pale yellow to gray markings. These spiders build irregular webs near the ground. Like black widows, false black widows hang upside down in their webs.

HOW TO SPOT

Size: 0.12 to 0.3 inches (3 to 7.6 mm) long

North American Range: States along the Pacific, Gulf, and Atlantic coasts

Habitat: Homes and other structures; on leaves or under bark

Diet: Insects and other spiders, including black widow spiders

Spiderling

Female

NORTHERN BLACK WIDOW

(LATRODECTUS VARIOLUS)

The northern black widow has a shiny black body. It has red or orange spots on its abdomen. It can have several white stripes as well. The underside of the abdomen has a red, orange, or yellowish hourglass marking. The marking is usually split in the middle or incomplete. Female northern black widows build tangled webs. Bites are rarely fatal. They are most dangerous to children. If disturbed, the spider tries to run away before biting.

HOW TO SPOT

Size: 0.2 to 0.5 inches (5 to 13 mm) long

North American Range: Southeastern Canada and the eastern half of the United States

Habitat: Outdoors in old stumps, hollow logs, abandoned animal burrows, rock piles, and brush piles and indoors in sheds, houses, and barns

Diet: Insects including fire ants, boll weevils, beetles, and grasshoppers

Female

STICKY SNARES

Many widow spiders build cobwebs with threads covered in a sticky glue. These threads stretch from the web to the ground and act as trip wires. When prey touches the threads, it is snapped upward into the web.

RED WIDOW *(LATRODECTUS BISHOPI)*

The red widow has a bright reddish-orange cephalothorax and legs. Its abdomen is shiny black. It has orange, red, or black spots with white outlines. The underside has one or two small red marks. These spiders usually make their funnel-shaped webs in unopened palmetto fronds. They loosely spin wider loops of strands at the tips of the fronds. These are called snare lines. Prey flies into the snare lines and falls into the web.

FUN FACT

Many female widow spiders eat their mates. A male red widow spider often places himself in the female's mouth. If she doesn't eat him right away, he keeps trying until she does.

HOW TO SPOT

Size: 0.1 to 0.3 inches (2.5 to 7.6 mm) long

North American Range: Central and southeastern Florida

Habitat: Open sandy areas with tall pines, short oaks, palmetto trees, and small plants

Diet: Flying insects and Florida scarab beetles

SOUTHERN BLACK WIDOW

(LATRODECTUS MACTANS)

The southern black widow has a shiny black body. The female has red spots on her abdomen. The male has red and white spots. Underneath is a red or orange hourglass marking. Some southern black widows build small silk funnels or tents. They can use them as retreats from danger or bad weather. The female stands guard over the eggs after mating. This is when most human bites happen.

HOW TO SPOT

Size: 0.16 to 0.5 inches (4 to 13 mm) long

North American Range: Southeastern United States

Habitat: Outdoors under stones, in stumps, and in woodpiles and indoors in houses, garages, sheds, and barns

Diet: Scorpions and insects including fire ants, boll weevils, grasshoppers, and beetles

Female, *top*, and male, *bottom*

FUN FACT

The venom of a black widow spider is 15 times more poisonous than that of a rattlesnake. But a spider can inject only a small amount of venom. This makes its bite much less serious.

TRIANGULATE COBWEB SPIDER

(STEATODA TRIANGULOSA)

Triangulate cobweb spiders are also called cupboard spiders. They have round abdomens with dark triangle-shaped designs. Females build irregular, tangled webs. These can be found along walls and under cabinets. The spider hangs upside down in its web. It rebuilds all or most of its web every day. After mating, the female makes egg sacs. The egg sacs look like round white puffballs. They can contain up to 30 eggs each.

HOW TO SPOT

Size: 0.06 to 0.25 inches (1.5 to 6.4 mm) long

North American Range: Southern Ontario in Canada and throughout the United States

Habitat: Houses, outbuildings, and sheds and under stones

Diet: Small insects and other arthropods, including ticks, spiders, and pill bugs

Female with egg sacs

WESTERN BLACK WIDOW

(LATRODECTUS HESPERUS)

Female western black widow spiders usually have a red hourglass shape on the underside of their abdomens, though the shape can also be a rectangle or dots. Males have an orange or yellow hourglass. The females build irregular, sticky webs. The female makes a yellowish egg sac that can contain up to 300 eggs. Females protect their eggs until the spiderlings leave. A western black widow may bite if someone comes near the egg sac.

HOW TO SPOT

Size: 0.13 to 0.33 inches (3.2 to 8.5 mm) long

North American Range: Western Canada, western United States, and Mexico

Habitat: Around homes, garages, and sheds in dark, sheltered areas such as buckets, garbage cans, pipes, and drains, and outside in holes and crevices

Diet: Insects such as beetles and flies, lizards, snakes, and small mammals

Female, *left*, and male, *right*

AMERICAN GREEN CRAB SPIDER *(MISUMESSUS OBLONGUS)*

The American green crab spider has a pale green cephalothorax and legs. Its abdomen is creamy white. Males often have a red stripe on the sides of their abdomens. This spider can wait for hours to ambush its prey. Then it uses its long front legs to grab the prey. The female lays her eggs in an egg sac. She folds a leaf over the sac to protect it. Then she closes it with silk.

FUN FACT

Crab spiders are named for their crab-like traits. They hold their long front legs open in front of their bodies so they can easily grab prey. They use their back legs to walk sideways or backward.

HOW TO SPOT

Size: 0.1 to 0.23 inches (2.6 to 6 mm) long

North American Range: Southeastern Canada, throughout the United States, and northern Mexico

Habitat: Fields, woodlands, and prairies

Diet: Other spiders and insects such as bees, butterflies, and beetles

BARK CRAB SPIDER

(BASSANIANA VERSICOLOR)

The bark crab spider has a flat cephalothorax. The abdomen is wide and flat. This spider has a dark body covered with light brown or white marks. These patterns help it blend into wood and tree bark. The bark crab spider can move around on trees looking for insects to eat. It can ambush prey by hiding under stones or wood. The spider grabs its prey with its long front legs and bites it.

HOW TO SPOT

Size: 0.15 to 0.3 inches (3.9 to 7.7 mm) long

North American Range: Throughout the United States except the northwestern states

Habitat: Woods, forests, and parks

Diet: Small insects

ELEGANT CRAB SPIDER

(XYSTICUS ELEGANS)

Elegant crab spiders are usually gray or brown. They have yellow, tan, and white markings. These spiders blend into the forest floor. For this reason, elegant crab spiders are sometimes called ground crab spiders. Elegant crab spiders can remain motionless for long periods of time. This helps them ambush their prey.

Female with egg sac

HOW TO SPOT

Size: 0.22 to 0.4 inches (5.5 to 10 mm) long

North American Range: Southern Canada and eastern United States

Habitat: On the forest floor under leaf litter, under logs and stones, and on foliage near the ground

Diet: Insects and other spiders

GOLDENROD CRAB SPIDER

(MISUMENA VATIA)

The female goldenrod crab spider is pale with orange or red stripes on her abdomen. The male is darker. These spiders do not spin webs. Like other crab spiders, goldenrod crab spiders are ambush hunters. The females can change colors between white and yellow. That way, they can blend in better with the flowers they are sitting on while waiting for prey.

HOW TO SPOT

Size: 0.12 to 0.35 inches (3 to 9 mm) long

North American Range: Throughout Canada and the United States

Habitat: Grasslands, prairies, and meadows

Diet: Insects such as flies, butterflies, grasshoppers, and bees

NORTHERN CRAB SPIDER

(MECAPHESA ASPERATA)

The northern crab spider can be white, yellow, or pale green. Its color can change to blend in with plants. It has reddish-brown markings. Spines on its body and legs make it look hairy. The northern crab spider waits on flowers for hours to ambush its prey. After mating, the female lays her eggs in the fold of a leaf. She guards the eggs until the spiderlings hatch.

HOW TO SPOT

Size: 0.14 to 0.28 inches (3.5 to 7 mm) long

North American Range: Southern Canada, throughout the United States, and Mexico

Habitat: Meadows, fields, roadsides, and gardens

Diet: Insects such as aphids, spider mites, moths, bees, wasps, and flies that visit flowering plants

SWIFT CRAB SPIDER

(MECAPHESA CELER)

The swift crab spider is white to yellow. It has dark stripes on the cephalothorax and a dark pattern on the abdomen. It also has hairs on its body and legs. The swift crab spider is active mostly at night. Sometimes it uses its silk to tie several flower petals together to create a hideout where it waits. When prey comes by, the swift crab spider grabs it. These spiders often catch insects larger than themselves.

HOW TO SPOT

Size: 0.13 to 0.25 inches (3.3 to 6.4 mm) long

North American Range: Southern Canada, throughout the United States, and parts of Mexico

Habitat: On shrubs, flowers, and small trees in meadows, forests, fields, and sand dunes

Diet: Insects including flies, butterflies, dragonflies, grasshoppers, wasps, bees, and aphids

TUBERCULATED CRAB SPIDER

(TMARUS ANGULATUS)

Tuberculated crab spiders are dull brown with black markings. These spiders can be pale or dark. A bump-like structure lies near the end of the abdomen. From the side, it looks like a bud or a broken leaf stalk. This helps the spider camouflage itself when hunting. It waits on a stem or twig with its front four legs stretched straight out. The female uses her webbing to make an egg sac. She watches over it for about a month until the eggs hatch.

HOW TO SPOT

Size: 0.12 to 0.28 inches (3 to 7 mm) long

North American Range: Southern Canada and across the United States

Habitat: On stems and twigs in fields, meadows, and gardens

Diet: Insects including ants

WHITEBANDED CRAB SPIDER

(MISUMENOIDES FORMOSIPES)

The whitebanded crab spider gets its name from the color of its face. It has a small white ridge just below its eight eyes. This spider comes in a variety of colors. The female's cephalothorax can be white, yellow, or pink. The abdomen has a pattern of dark markings. The male's cephalothorax can be green, brown, yellow, or orange. The abdomen is usually yellow or orange too. The female whitebanded crab spider often changes color to blend in with its surroundings.

HOW TO SPOT

Size: 0.13 to 0.5 inches (3.3 to 13 mm) long

North American Range: Western Canada and throughout the United States

Habitat: On flowers in fields or bogs

Diet: Other spiders and insects such as bees and flies

HOBO SPIDER *(ERATIGENA AGRESTIS)*

Hobo spiders are native to Europe. They were first discovered in North America in 1936. The hobo spider has a brown body with dark markings on the legs and abdomen. Hobo spiders normally run away from threats. They bite only if there is no way to escape. The hobo spider cannot climb the smooth surfaces found indoors. For this reason, hobo spiders often get stuck in bathtubs and sinks.

HOW TO SPOT

Size: 0.31 to 0.6 inches (8 to 15 mm) long

North American Range: Western United States

Habitat: Sheltered areas such as wood and rock piles, tall grass, and retaining walls

Diet: Insects

PENNSYLVANIA GRASS SPIDER

(AGELENOPSIS PENNSYLVANICA)

The Pennsylvania grass spider has a grayish-brown body with dark and light stripes. It has long spinnerets at the end of its abdomen. These spiders build their webs near the ground. The webs are not sticky. They are built mostly horizontally like a sheet. As the weather becomes cooler, the spiders often move indoors. They crawl into homes and other structures.

HOW TO SPOT

Size: 0.35 to 0.8 inches (9 to 20 mm) long

North American Range: Throughout the United States except for the southwestern states

Habitat: Fencerows, bushes, brush piles, and ground cover such as dense grass and weeds around homes and yards

Diet: Small flying insects

PARSON SPIDER

(HERPYLLUS ECCLESIASTICUS)

The parson spider is a hairy, black spider. It has a white stripe on its abdomen that looks like a necktie. Parson spiders make silken lairs to hide in during the day. Outdoors, these webs can be between fallen leaves or pieces of loose bark. Indoors, the webs can be in the folds of clothing in drawers or closets. Parson spiders hunt at night on the ground and on walls.

HOW TO SPOT

Size: 0.23 to 0.5 inches (6 to 13 mm) long

North American Range: Throughout Canada, the United States, and Mexico

Habitat: Under rocks, stones, boards, and other debris in woodland areas and in homes and buildings

Diet: Insects and other spiders

VARIEGATED SPIDER

(SERGIOLUS CAPULATUS)

A variegated spider has an orange cephalothorax. The abdomen is black with white stripes. These spiders may be mistaken for velvet ants, a type of stinging wasp without wings. Variegated spiders are mostly active in the daytime. Sometimes they stalk their prey in leaf litter. They are also good climbers. They often climb on plants and walls. Variegated spiders use their webs for shelter. They guard egg sacs there too.

HOW TO SPOT

Size: 0.22 to 0.4 inches (5.5 to 10 mm) long

North American Range: United States from the Great Plains to the East Coast

Habitat: Under bark, leaf litter, stones, and woodpiles in grasslands, open areas, and woods

Diet: Small insects such as mites, aphids, and fruit flies

BLACK LACE WEAVER

(AMAUROBIUS FEROX)

Black lace weavers are native to Europe. These spiders spin irregular webs at night. When the webs are new, they look like lace. They are blue and very sticky. The strands surround a circular retreat. Males live only a few months. They die after they mate. Females can live about two years. The female lays her eggs in a sac inside the retreat.

Female near her retreat

HOW TO SPOT

Size: 0.33 to 0.6 inches (8.5 to 14 mm) long

North American Range: Southeastern Canada and eastern United States

Habitat: Under bark, leaf litter, woodpiles, stones, and other protected areas and in basements

Diet: Small insects

HACKLEMESH WEAVER

(CALLOBIUS BENNETTI)

The hacklemesh weaver has a shiny reddish-brown cephalothorax and a fuzzy abdomen. The abdomen has a light-colored pattern. These spiders make irregular webs in bark and woodpiles. They can also build their webs around porch lights, doorframes, and windows. The web has a funnel-shaped retreat. When the weather becomes cold, the spiders may move indoors. After mating, the male dies. The female makes an egg sac. The egg sac is often attached to the web.

HOW TO SPOT

Size: 0.2 to 0.6 inches (5 to 14 mm) long

North American Range: Eastern Canada and northeastern United States

Habitat: Outdoors under bark, leaf litter, stones, and woodpiles and indoors in damp basements

Diet: Small insects and other arthropods

ANT-MIMICKING JUMPING SPIDER *(MYRMARACHNE FORMICARIA)*

The ant-mimicking jumping spider is native to Europe and Asia. These jumping spiders look like ants. They also move like ants. As they walk, they pause to raise their front two legs in the air. These legs look like an ant's antennae. The ant-mimicking jumping spider walks a winding path like an ant. The spiders can fool predators. Ants are aggressive and taste bad to most predators. So predators avoid these jumping spiders too.

HOW TO SPOT

Size: Average 0.23 inches (6 mm) long

North American Range: Ontario in Canada to Ohio, Pennsylvania, and New York in the United States

Habitat: Near ant colonies

Diet: Insects such as small flies and mosquitoes

APACHE JUMPING SPIDER

(PHIDIPPUS APACHEANUS)

The Apache jumping spider is black with orange on top of the cephalothorax and abdomen. Its coloring looks similar to that of the velvet ant, which has a painful sting. The spider's bright colors likely protect it from predators. The male performs a long courtship dance to attract a mate. If the female accepts him, she performs a dance as well.

HOW TO SPOT

Size: 0.2 to 0.5 inches (5.2 to 13 mm) long

North American Range: Southwestern United States

Habitat: Dry grasslands, fields, deserts, and around homes and farms including by fence posts, barns, and roads

Diet: Insects including flies, butterflies, moths, and beetles

BOLD JUMPER *(PHIDIPPUS AUDAX)*

The bold jumper is a black, hairy spider. It has a pattern of white, yellow, or orange spots on the top of its abdomen. Males have tufts of hairs over their eyes that look like eyebrows. Like most jumping spiders, bold jumpers hunt alone during the day. They watch for prey with their sharp eyesight. Then they pounce on it. Bold jumpers quickly jump away from potential predators.

HOW TO SPOT

Size: 0.23 to 0.6 inches (6 to 15 mm) long

North American Range: Southern Canada, throughout the United States, and northern Mexico

Habitat: Grasslands, prairies, open woodlands, fields, backyards, gardens, and buildings

Diet: Other spiders and insects including boll weevils and moths

BRONZE JUMPER *(ERIS MILITARIS)*

Bronze jumpers are small to medium brown spiders. Each side of the cephalothorax has a white stripe. The abdomen has a white stripe around it. These spiders prefer open, sunny places. They are often found crawling on building walls. In the fall, groups of bronze jumpers gather in the same place, such as under tree bark. They may spend the winter together. They come out in early spring and summer.

HOW TO SPOT

Size: 0.2 to 0.31 inches (5 to 8 mm) long

North American Range: Throughout most of Canada and the United States

Habitat: Sunny areas with trees and low vegetation; human structures

Diet: Small insects

SUPER VISION

Jumping spiders have the best eyesight of all spiders. The two main forward-facing eyes see in high-detail color. The next pair sees in black and white. The other eyes have less detailed vision in black and white. When all eight eyes work together, the spider has a nearly 360-degree view. With such sharp eyesight, jumping spiders can stalk and pounce on their prey with precision.

CANOPY JUMPING SPIDER

(PHIDIPPUS OTIOSUS)

The canopy jumping spider is one of the largest jumping spiders in North America. There are several variations in color. Most are black with white or cream-colored hair. In Florida, these spiders often have yellow to orange hair. Most canopy jumping spiders have metallic-green mouthparts. Some can have purple mouthparts instead. Like other jumping spiders, the canopy jumping spider stalks its prey. Then it pounces on the prey.

HOW TO SPOT

Size: 0.31 to 0.7 inches (8 to 18 mm) long

North American Range: Along the US East Coast and southeastern United States

Habitat: Treetops in deciduous and evergreen forests

Diet: Insects

COMMON HENTZ JUMPING SPIDER *(HENTZIA PALMARUM)*

The female common Hentz jumping spider has a yellowish body with dark markings. It is covered with white hairs. Males are a much darker reddish brown. They have a white stripe around the head and abdomen. The male's first pair of legs is dark red and much longer than the others. Common Hentz jumping spiders have two large, round eyes in the front of their faces. These are surrounded by six smaller eyes.

Male

Female

HOW TO SPOT

Size: 0.16 to 0.28 inches (4 to 7 mm) long

North American Range: The United States from Texas to the southeast and into Mexico

Habitat: Shrubs and small trees

Diet: Insects and other spiders

DIMORPHIC JUMPING SPIDER

(MAEVIA INCLEMENS)

The dimorphic jumping spider is the only jumping spider species with two colors of males. Some males have a dark brown or black body and pale yellow legs. The cephalothorax has three small tufts of black hair. Other males are lighter. They have gray bodies with red, white, and black markings. The females look like these males but with orange or red stripes. The two types of males perform different mating dances.

Dark male

HOW TO SPOT

Size: 0.19 to 0.4 inches (4.8 to 10 mm) long

North American Range: Central and eastern Canada and United States

Habitat: Along tree lines and trails in vines and ivy, in shrubs and grasses, and on human structures including fences and outbuildings

Diet: Small insects and other arthropods

Gray male

EMERALD JUMPING SPIDER

(PARAPHIDIPPUS AURANTIUS)

The emerald jumping spider is medium to large in size. Both males and females have a shiny green iridescence. Some spiders appear more golden than green. The spider's shiny colors seem to change when light hits its body from different angles. The abdomen has eight white spots. It also has orange spots on the sides. The emerald jumping spider builds a retreat for shelter. It is made with silk and a folded leaf.

HOW TO SPOT

Size: 0.28 to 0.5 inches (7 to 12 mm) long

North American Range: Midwestern, eastern, and southern United States

Habitat: Rural and suburban wooded locations and open areas of shrubs and grasses

Diet: Insects and other spiders

Male

Female

GRAY WALL JUMPING SPIDER

(MENEMERUS BIVITTATUS)

Gray wall jumping spiders originally came from tropical areas in Africa. The male's abdomen has black in the center with gray on the sides. The female has gray in the center with black on the sides. Gray wall jumping spiders hunt mostly during the day. However, they are often found around lights at night. They catch insects attracted to the lights.

FUN FACT

Jumping spiders add pressure to their legs by pushing special fluid into them. This causes their legs to straighten out very quickly, letting the spiders jump far and high.

HOW TO SPOT

Size: 0.31 to 0.4 inches (8 to 10 mm) long

North American Range: California to North Carolina and Florida

Habitat: Vertical surfaces such as outdoor walls

Diet: Small flying insects including flies and mosquitoes

MAGNOLIA GREEN JUMPING SPIDER *(LYSSOMANES VIRIDIS)*

The magnolia green jumping spider is bright green. It has an orange or red marking on its head. There are small black dots on the abdomen. These spiders have long, thin legs. The front eyes are unusually large. These eyes appear green from the side. But when the spider looks directly at someone, they appear black. Females lay their eggs on the undersides of leaves. They cover the eggs with silk.

Female

HOW TO SPOT

Size: 0.2 to 0.31 inches (5 to 8 mm) long

North American Range: Southern United States

Habitat: Woods and forests on trees including magnolias, oaks, maples, and pines

Diet: Other small jumping spiders and plant-eating insects including aphids, mites, and ants

Male

SILK FOR SAFETY

Before leaping, a jumping spider attaches itself to an object with a silk thread. This thread is called a dragline. If the spider misses its target or falls, the dragline catches the spider. Then the spider just climbs back up.

REGAL JUMPING SPIDER

(PHIDIPPUS REGIUS)

The regal jumping spider is one of the largest jumping spiders. Males are black with white markings on their legs and abdomens. Females are covered with colored scales. They can be any combination of gray, tan, brown, or orange. Females make thick nests under tree bark to lay their eggs. They can also use cracks in old houses and barns. Females can produce multiple egg sacs, each with 50 to 200 eggs.

HOW TO SPOT

Size: 0.23 to 0.9 inches (6 to 22 mm) long

North American Range: Southeastern United States

Habitat: Gardens, fields, open woodlands, and on the walls of buildings

Diet: Small insects and other arthropods

ZEBRA SPIDER *(SALTICUS SCENICUS)*

The zebra spider is native to Europe. It has three to four white stripes on its abdomen. The zebra spider wanders alone. It builds a small silk shelter under leaves, stones, or tree bark. Zebra spiders often hunt on outside walls in sunny areas. These spiders are curious. They approach almost anything that moves. Like other jumping spiders, they stalk their prey. Once they are close enough, they pounce on it.

HOW TO SPOT

Size: 0.16 to 0.28 inches (4 to 7 mm) long

North American Range: Southern Canada to Mexico

Habitat: Forests, meadows, gardens, and human structures such as walls, fences, and windowpanes

Diet: Small spiders and insects such as mosquitoes, flies, butterflies, moths, ants, wasps, and bees

GREEN LYNX SPIDER

(PEUCETIA VIRIDANS)

The green lynx spider is the largest lynx spider in North America. It has a bright green body that can turn brown or yellow when resting. Its long, thin legs are spotted and spiny. Green lynx spiders use their silk to build platforms for hunting. They wait for prey to come close. They can also stalk their prey. After mating, the female makes an egg sac. She guards her young until they leave, about ten days after hatching.

HOW TO SPOT

Size: 0.5 to 0.9 inches (12 to 22 mm) long

North American Range: Southern United States to Mexico and Central America

Habitat: Gardens, meadows, and fields

Diet: Insects such as moths, butterflies, bees, wasps, flies, and grasshoppers

STRIPED LYNX SPIDER

(OXYOPES SALTICUS)

The striped lynx spider has black markings on its face. It has long black spines on its legs. Lynx spiders have eight eyes. Six of the eyes form a hexagon shape at the top of the head. Two smaller eyes are located on the front of the face. Lynx spiders get their name from the cat-like ways they hunt. Sometimes they approach their prey very slowly. Other times, they lie in wait and then pounce on their prey.

HOW TO SPOT

Size: 0.15 to 0.3 inches (3.7 to 7.4 mm) long

North American Range: The West Coast and eastern states in the United States, Mexico, and Central America

Habitat: Prairies, backyards, gardens, and cotton, soybean, and alfalfa fields

Diet: Other spiders and insects such as leafhoppers, stink bugs, bollworms, and aphids

AMERICAN NURSERY WEB SPIDER *(PISAURINA MIRA)*

The American nursery web spider can be tan, brown, or gray. It has a wide brown stripe down the middle of its back. These spiders often hold their front two pairs of legs together when resting. They move slowly among the grass to search for prey. The female carries her egg sac with her. Right before the spiderlings emerge, she builds a tangled web, called a nursery web, to keep them safe while hatching.

HOW TO SPOT

Size: 0.35 to 0.6 inches (9 to 15 mm) long

North American Range: Midwestern and eastern United States

Habitat: Fields, meadows, prairies, and woods with tall grasses and shrubs

Diet: Small insects such as gnats and mosquitoes

FUN FACT

Spiders have many different types of courtship rituals. The male American nursery web spider offers the female a gift of an insect wrapped in silk.

Female with spiderlings in nursery web

DARK FISHING SPIDER

(DOLOMEDES TENEBROSUS)

Dark fishing spiders are brown to gray. They have three W-shaped marks on their abdomens. Their legs have brown and black stripes and long spines. These spiders hunt at night. They pounce on prey. The female spider lays 1,000 or more eggs in an egg sac. She carries the egg sac until the eggs are ready to hatch. The female guards the spiderlings in a nursery web. She watches over them until they leave.

HOW TO SPOT

Size: 0.23 to 1 inch (6 to 25 mm) long

North American Range: Canada and eastern United States

Habitat: Dry wooded areas; around rocks, shrubs, and logs in yards; and in homes

Diet: Insects and other small arthropods

DIVING DEEP

Fishing spiders can dive underwater to catch prey. They can go as deep as seven inches (18 cm). They can also dive to avoid a predator. Water-repellent hairs on the body trap air around the spider. A fishing spider breathes this air. It can stay underwater for up to 30 minutes.

SIX-SPOTTED FISHING SPIDER

(DOLOMEDES TRITON)

The six-spotted fishing spider has a brown abdomen with white spots. It gets its name from the six dark spots on the underside of the abdomen. These spiders eat many foods. Sometimes they hunt on land. They search for prey along the shoreline. They also hunt on the surface of the water. Six-spotted fishing spiders can walk or run across the water. They use their legs to push themselves along.

HOW TO SPOT

Size: 0.35 to 1 inch (9 to 26 mm) long

North American Range: Midwestern and eastern United States to Mexico and Central America

Habitat: Around ponds, slow-moving streams, swampy areas, and other damp places

Diet: Aquatic insects, tadpoles, and tiny fish

WHITE-BANDED FISHING SPIDER *(DOLOMEDES ALBINEUS)*

The white-banded fishing spider has a white to greenish-gray body with dark markings. Tufts of white hairs on the legs make them appear fuzzy. The spider is named for a white band on its face. These spiders are usually found sitting head down on walls or tree trunks. They rarely hunt on the water. Like other fishing spiders, the female makes a nursery web. Then she guards the egg sac and the spiderlings.

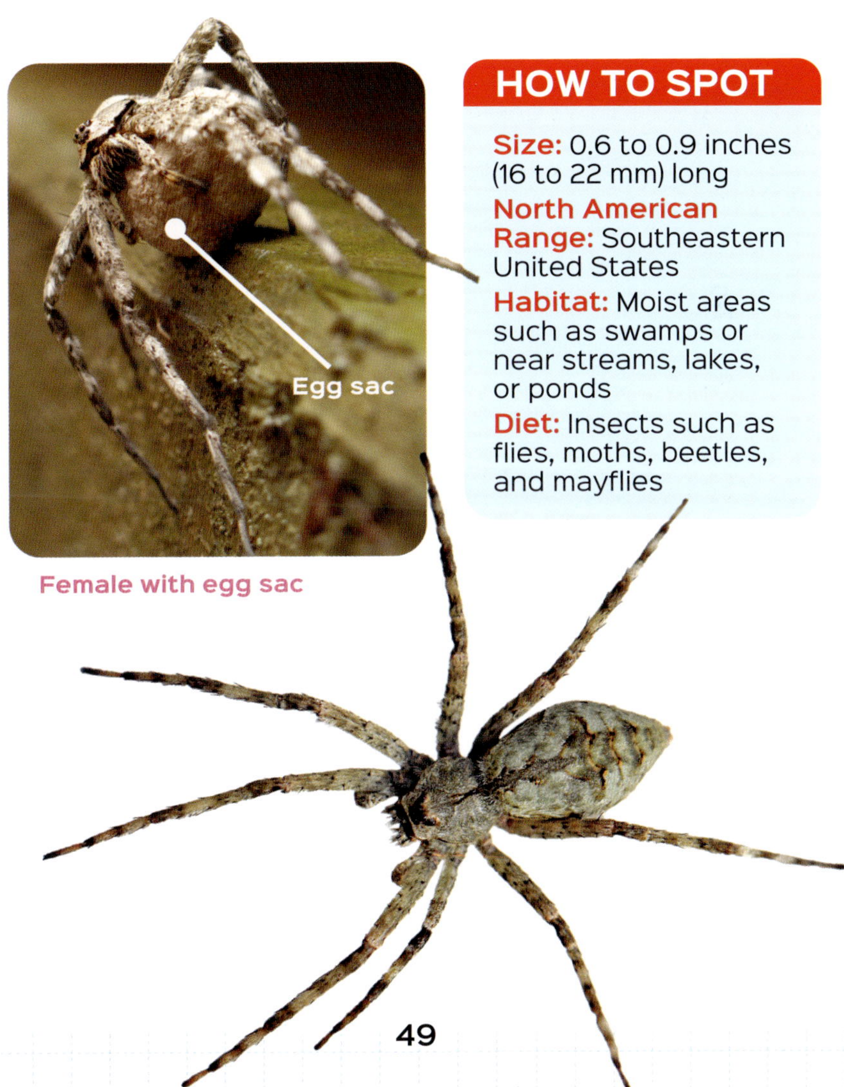

Female with egg sac

HOW TO SPOT

Size: 0.6 to 0.9 inches (16 to 22 mm) long

North American Range: Southeastern United States

Habitat: Moist areas such as swamps or near streams, lakes, or ponds

Diet: Insects such as flies, moths, beetles, and mayflies

ARABESQUE ORB WEAVER

(NEOSCONA ARABESCA)

The arabesque orb weaver ranges from tan to yellow, orange, or brown. The abdomen has slanting dark marks. These lines are sometimes surrounded by a white patch. This pattern looks like an arabesque, which is a swirling design often used in art. At night, the female spider spins a web to catch insects. By morning, the web is damaged. The female eats the web. She spins a new one the next night.

HOW TO SPOT

Size: 0.17 to 0.5 inches (4.2 to 12 mm) long

North American Range: Throughout North America from Canada to Central America

Habitat: Grasslands, woodlands, meadows, gardens, and on the outsides of buildings

Diet: Flying insects such as moths and flies

ARROWHEAD SPIDER

(VERRUCOSA ARENATA)

The arrowhead spider is also known as the triangle orb weaver. Its abdomen is white or bright yellow. The female's abdomen is pointy and shaped like the tip of an arrow. Males do not have this feature. Like other orb weavers, arrowhead spiders spin circular webs. The sticky strands catch insects. The webs are small and delicate. Most orb weavers sit head down in their webs. But arrowhead spiders sit with their heads up.

HOW TO SPOT

Size: Up to 0.38 inches (9.7 mm) long

North American Range: Across North America

Habitat: Woods, hiking trails, yards, wetlands, gardens, and marshes

Diet: Insects, especially tiny flying insects such as mosquitoes

WEB SIGNALS

Spiders do not have ears. Some spiders sense vibrations instead. First, the spider plucks a strand of its web. Vibrations go out in every direction along the web. The spider can sense the vibrations in its legs. The vibrations tell the spider where prey is caught. They also tell the spider if the web needs repairs.

ARROWSHAPED MICRATHENA

(MICRATHENA SAGITTATA)

Arrowshaped micrathenas are small spiders. The male is dark and rarely seen. The female is easier to spot. Her abdomen is bright yellow with two long spikes at the back. The spikes have black tips. Arrowshaped micrathenas are active during the day. The female spiders make webs with closely spaced circles to catch small insects. The male visits the female in the web to mate.

HOW TO SPOT

Size: 0.16 to 0.35 inches (4 to 9 mm) long

North American Range: Eastern United States

Habitat: In yards, along the edges of woods, in forests, and in brushy areas

Diet: Insects such as beetles, flies, wasps, ants, mosquitoes, and leafhoppers

FUN FACT

Some people think the arrowshaped micrathena resembles the cartoon character Pikachu.

BANDED GARDEN SPIDER

(ARGIOPE TRIFASCIATA)

The female banded garden spider has many thin silver, yellow, and black lines on her abdomen. The cephalothorax is covered with silvery hairs. The male's abdomen is mostly white. This spider spins large, spiral-shaped webs. It usually makes a zigzag pattern in the middle of the web. The spider removes dead insects and damaged silk from its web. This keeps the web in good condition.

HOW TO SPOT

Size: 0.16 to 1 inch (4 to 25 mm) long

North American Range: Southern Canada and throughout the United States

Habitat: Fields, gardens, and other dry open areas

Diet: Flying insects such as grasshoppers, cicadas, katydids, flies, bees, and butterflies

BARN SPIDER *(ARANEUS CAVATICUS)*

Barn spiders are a dull brown or gray. Their legs are striped. Near the front of the abdomen are two humps. They look like shoulders. Underneath the abdomen is one large black spot and two small white spots. The spider's whole body is hairy. The female barn spider builds a new web every evening. The webs can be large. Strands can extend up to 10 feet (3 m).

HOW TO SPOT

Size: 0.4 to 0.9 inches (10 to 22 mm) long

North American Range: Northeastern Canada south to Texas

Habitat: Caves, cliff overhangs, and shady areas in human structures such as under the edges of roofs, on porches, or in barns

Diet: Insects

Underside of abdomen

FUN FACT

The spider in the book *Charlotte's Web* by E. B. White is a barn spider.

CAT-FACED SPIDER

(ARANEUS GEMMOIDES)

The cat-faced spider gets its name from the pattern on its abdomen. Two humps near the front of the top of the abdomen resemble a cat's ears. Dimples in the abdomen look like a cat's eyes. A faint white line runs down the middle of the abdomen. This is usually crossed with two small V-shaped markings. In the fall, the female makes an egg sac before she dies. Only the eggs survive the winter.

HOW TO SPOT

Size: 0.2 to 1 inch (5 to 25 mm) long

North American Range: Southern Canada and western and central United States

Habitat: Around buildings, cliffs, cave entrances, and pine forests

Diet: Garden and flying insects

CROSS ORB WEAVER

(ARANEUS DIADEMATUS)

The cross orb weaver is native to Europe. This spider's color can range from pale yellow to brown to black. The abdomen has two wavy lines and white or yellow spots. Four long spots near the front of the abdomen form a cross-like pattern. The cross orb weaver spins a new web every day. If the spider feels threatened, it might use its legs to shake its web and scare away the threat.

FUN FACT

In 1973 a high school student worked with the US National Aeronautics and Space Administration to send cross orb weavers into space. They were placed aboard the Skylab 3 mission. The spiders could still build webs in zero gravity.

HOW TO SPOT

Size: 0.22 to 0.8 inches (5.5 to 20 mm) long

North American Range: Southern Canada and across the northern United States

Habitat: Woodlands, savannas, meadows, gardens, grasslands, evergreen forests, and buildings and homes, especially ones with outdoor lighting

Diet: Insects

FEATHER-LEGGED ORB WEAVER *(ULOBORUS GLOMOSUS)*

Feather-legged orb weavers are small, hairy spiders. They can be tan, gray, or brown. The female has tufts of feather-like hair on her first pair of legs. This spider makes circular, horizontal webs. The webs do not have sticky threads. Instead, woolly fuzz on the strands traps prey. After mating, the female attaches the egg sacs in a straight line on a silk thread. The female rests at one end.

HOW TO SPOT

Size: Up to 0.25 inches (6.4 mm) long

North American Range: Eastern Canada and United States

Habitat: Low shrubs and other vegetation

Diet: Flies, mosquitoes, and other small insects

GOLDEN SILK ORB WEAVER

(TRICHONEPHILA CLAVIPES)

The golden silk orb weaver gets its name from its yellow silk. Females are usually yellow, white, and black. They have two hairy black bands on each leg. The males are dark brown. The females make huge webs that can span more than 3 feet (0.9 m) across. The web has two parts. Prey is caught on a classic round web. A second tangled web off to one side vibrates when predators approach, alerting the spider.

HOW TO SPOT

Size: 0.23 to 1.5 inches (6 to 38 mm) long

North American Range: Southeastern United States

Habitat: Open woods, forest edges, trails, and citrus groves

Diet: Small-to-medium-sized flying insects such as bees, wasps, flies, horseflies, moths, and butterflies

Undersides of male, *top*, and female, *bottom*

SEVEN SILKS

There are seven different types of spider silk. Some are strong, and some are sticky. Each one serves a different purpose. Golden silk orb weavers can produce all seven types of silk.

HENTZ ORB WEAVER

(NEOSCONA CRUCIFERA)

The Hentz orb weaver is reddish brown to brown. Its web can be nearly 2 feet (60 cm) across. The spider makes a retreat of leaves tied with silk. During the day, the spider stays in the retreat. It sits in the center of the web at night. The female spider creates egg sacs made of fluffy yellow threads. These are rolled up in a leaf.

HOW TO SPOT

Size: 0.18 to 0.8 inches (4.5 to 20 mm) long

North American Range: Central, eastern, and southwestern United States into Mexico

Habitat: Moist open woods and gardens and under overhanging roofs of houses and buildings in wooded areas

Diet: Insects

WEB RECYCLING

Wind, rain, and prey can damage a spider's web. Some species of orb weavers build new webs every day. First, they tear down their old webs. Then they eat most of the silk. That way, they reuse some of the proteins and other nutrients from the silk to build new webs. They also get moisture from any dew that might be on the webs.

HUMPED TRASHLINE ORB WEAVER *(CYCLOSA TURBINATA)*

The humped trashline orb weaver has a dark brown cephalothorax. The abdomen is brown and white. There are two humps on the abdomen. This spider builds a small, circular web. The spider uses silk to wrap the dried bodies of insects it has eaten. It also wraps other bits of debris. Then it attaches them to a line of silk across the web. The spider rests in the center of the line. It blends in with the debris.

Humped trashline orb weaver

HOW TO SPOT

Size: 0.14 to 0.3 inches (3.6 to 7.5 mm) long

North American Range: Central and southern North America

Habitat: Wooded areas including parks and yards and sides of buildings near the foundations

Diet: Small flying insects including mosquitoes, midges, moths, small beetles, and houseflies

LONG-JAWED ORB WEAVER

(TETRAGNATHA VERSICOLOR)

Long-jawed orb weavers range from tan to dark brown. Their jaws are long compared to those of other orb weavers. Their abdomens are long and thin. These spiders are sometimes called "stretch spiders." They often stretch their legs out flat. The spiders look like the sticks they are resting on. This offers camouflage from predators. These spiders spin circular webs over the water's surface. They use their webs to catch prey.

HOW TO SPOT

Size: 0.17 to 0.5 inches (4.3 to 13 mm) long

North American Range: Across North America

Habitat: Shrubs and trees that hang over bodies of water and the sides of docks and piers

Diet: Small flying insects including mayflies, midges, stoneflies, and lacewings

MARBLED ORB WEAVER

(ARANEUS MARMOREUS)

Female marbled orb weavers have large, round abdomens. These can be white, yellow, or orange. They have brown, purple, and pale yellow markings. The web's sticky spiral threads catch prey. The marbled orb weaver makes a retreat of leaves and silk off to the side. The spider waits in the retreat. When a thread attached to the center of the web vibrates, the spider knows it may have caught an insect.

HOW TO SPOT

Size: 0.2 to 0.7 inches (5 to 18 mm) long

North American Range: Throughout Canada and the United States

Habitat: Trees, shrubs, tall weeds, and grasses in forests, meadows, fields, neighborhoods, and orchards, and along rivers and streams

Diet: Small insects

ORCHARD ORB WEAVER

(LEUCAUGE VENUSTA)

The orchard orb weaver is part of a group known as the long-jawed orb weavers. These spiders have long bodies, legs, and jaws. The abdomen of the orchard orb weaver is usually silvery white. It can also have green, brown, red, or yellow markings. The orchard orb weaver makes a new web each morning. The web has 30 or more spokes stretching from the center. The outside of the web contains about 60 sticky circles to catch prey.

FUN FACT

Orchard orb weavers can tell the difference between vibrations in their webs. They ignore vibrations made by an angry bee. But they respond to those made by a fly.

HOW TO SPOT

Size: 0.14 to 0.3 inches (3.5 to 7.5 mm) long

North American Range: Southern Canada, eastern United States to Georgia, and Southern California

Habitat: Citrus groves, woodland edges, meadows, gardens, tree lines, hedges and shrubs, and shaded areas of houses and other structures

Diet: Small insects such as mosquitoes, flies, and gnats

SILVER ARGIOPE

(ARGIOPE ARGENTATA)

The silver argiope has a bumpy abdomen with yellow, orange, and black markings. Its silvery color comes from reflective silver hairs. The spider builds its web between cacti or other plants. Part of the web is a zigzag pattern called a stabilimentum. Scientists are still trying to understand the use of this feature. The silver argiope makes four of these patterns in a cross shape.

HOW TO SPOT

Size: 0.16 to 0.5 inches (4 to 12 mm) long

North American Range: Southern North America

Habitat: Parks, gardens, fields, woods, and other open areas with plants

Diet: Insects

SPINY-BACKED ORB WEAVER

(GASTERACANTHA CANCRIFORMIS)

The female spiny-backed orb weaver has a colorful abdomen. It can be white, yellow, or orange with black spots. It has sharp spines that stick outward. These have black or red tips. The spines help scare away predators. The males have gray and white markings and shorter spikes. They are very small and rarely seen. Males die soon after mating. The female dies after attaching the egg sac to the underside of a leaf.

HOW TO SPOT

Size: 0.08 to 0.35 inches (2 to 9 mm) long

North American Range: Southern United States from California to Florida and south to Central America

Habitat: Grasses, trees, and shrubs in neighborhoods, gardens, forest edges, and citrus groves

Diet: Insects such as flies, beetles, moths, and mosquitoes

TOADLIKE BOLAS SPIDER

(MASTOPHORA PHRYNOSOMA)

The toadlike bolas spider has a bumpy brown, gray, or white abdomen. It rests on a leaf during the day. It looks like a bird dropping. Predators do not notice it. At night, the spider makes a sticky silk ball and string called a bolas. The string attaches to one of its legs. The spider releases a scent like a female moth. It attracts male moths. When a moth comes close, the spider flings the bolas to catch it.

HOW TO SPOT

Size: 0.06 to 0.5 inches (1.5 to 12 mm) long

North American Range: Eastern United States

Habitat: Shrubs and low tree branches

Diet: Moths and moth flies

FUN FACT

The small male toadlike bolas spiders do not hunt with a bolas. But they produce a scent that attracts tiny insects called moth flies. They grab the moth flies and eat them.

Toadlike bolas spider hunting with a bolas

YELLOW GARDEN SPIDER

(ARGIOPE AURANTIA)

Yellow garden spiders have black abdomens with bright orange or yellow markings. Short, silvery hairs cover the cephalothorax. The females are about three times larger than the males. The females spin large webs with a white zigzag stripe down the center. For this reason, they are sometimes called writing spiders.

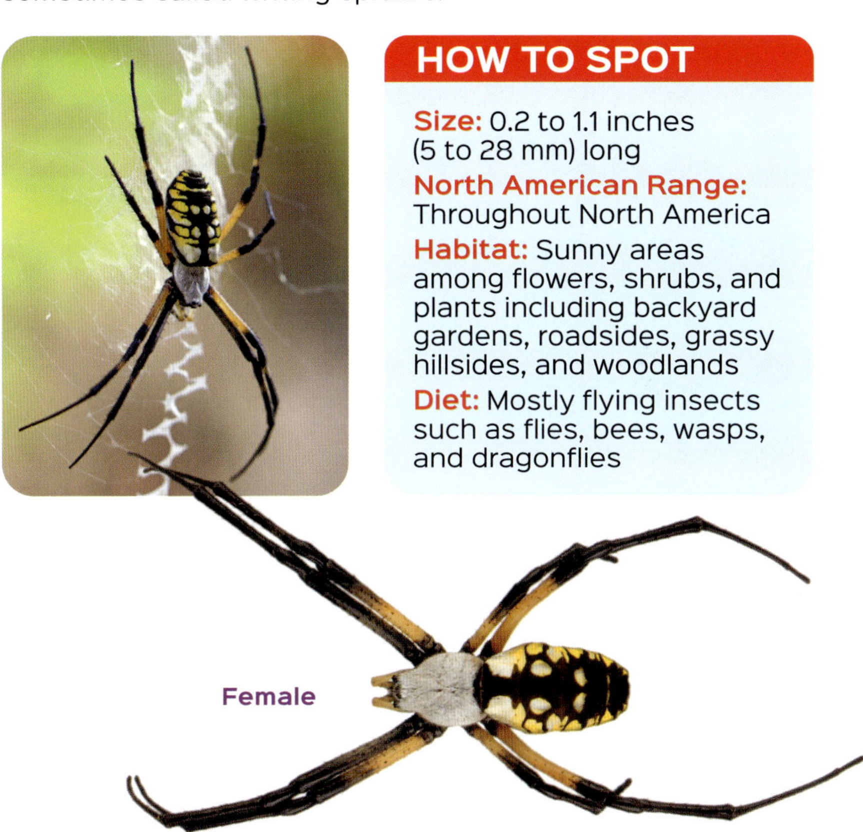

HOW TO SPOT

Size: 0.2 to 1.1 inches (5 to 28 mm) long

North American Range: Throughout North America

Habitat: Sunny areas among flowers, shrubs, and plants including backyard gardens, roadsides, grassy hillsides, and woodlands

Diet: Mostly flying insects such as flies, bees, wasps, and dragonflies

SHINY STRANDS

Ultraviolet (UV) light is a type of light humans cannot see. But insects are attracted to UV light. They use UV light to find flowers. Some spiders make webs with strands that reflect UV light. Insects are tricked into flying toward the webs.

BLUE PURSEWEB SPIDER

(SPHODROS ABBOTI)

The blue purseweb spider gets its name from the color of the male spider. It has a black cephalothorax and a shiny blue abdomen. The female has a dark brown cephalothorax and reddish- or purplish-brown abdomen. These spiders build tube-shaped webs against tree trunks. The webs begin belowground. They can extend up to about 14 inches (35 cm) up the tree. Blue purseweb spiders can live up to ten years.

FUN FACT

Purseweb spiders got their name in 1792. An artist and naturalist named John T. Abbot named them. He thought their webs looked like the purses that were in fashion at the time.

HOW TO SPOT

Size: Up to 0.7 inches (19 mm) long

North American Range: Southern Georgia and northern Florida

Habitat: Moist forests and swamps

Diet: Insects and other arthropods such as millipedes and smaller spiders

RED-LEGGED PURSEWEB SPIDER *(SPHODROS RUFIPES)*

Red-legged purseweb spiders have dark brown to black bodies. Females have brown legs. Males have bright orangish-red legs. The females build tube-shaped webs. They usually build their webs against small tree trunks. The web is often covered with debris. This helps camouflage it. The web is not sticky. The spider waits inside the tube for prey to cross the web. Then it pulls the prey through the side of the tube.

HOW TO SPOT

Size: 0.6 to 1 inch (15 to 25 mm) long

North American Range: Eastern United States and as far west as Texas

Habitat: Hardwood forests

Diet: Arthropods including millipedes, crickets, beetles, wasps, ants, caterpillars, and other spiders

Male

Female

BROWN RECLUSE

(LOXOSCELES RECLUSA)

The brown recluse spider can be pale tan to dark brown. It has a violin-shaped marking on its cephalothorax. This spider builds a silk retreat to hide in during the day. It can also hide in clothing or shoes. At night, the spider wanders out to find prey. If the spider is threatened, it usually runs away. A bite can require medical attention and in rare cases is deadly.

HOW TO SPOT

Size: 0.2 to 0.6 inches (5 to 15 mm) long

North American Range: Central and southern United States

Habitat: Cracks and crevices in and under rocks and log piles, under leaf litter, and in human environments such as under trash cans, wood, tarps, boxes, and tires

Diet: Small insects and other spiders

FUN FACT

Brown recluse spiders can go up to 12 months without food or water.

DESERT RECLUSE

(LOXOSCELES DESERTA)

The desert recluse spider is pale yellow to tan. Most desert recluse spiders have a very light marking shaped like a violin. Some spiders do not have the marking at all. Like other recluse spiders, the desert recluse has six eyes. The eyes are arranged in two rows. This spider spins irregularly shaped webs. Desert recluse spiders stay mostly outdoors under rocks or other debris.

HOW TO SPOT

Size: 0.25 to 0.5 inches (6.4 to 13 mm) long

North American Range: The Mojave and Sonoran Deserts in California, Nevada, Utah, and Arizona and northwestern Mexico

Habitat: Deserts and other dry environments

Diet: Small, live insects and sometimes large, dead insects

BROAD-FACED SAC SPIDER

(TRACHELAS TRANQUILLUS)

The broad-faced sac spider has a pale yellow, tan, or gray abdomen with a stripe down the middle. The cephalothorax is dark red. Broad-faced sac spiders usually stay outdoors. They hide in their silken retreats during the day. These can be at the base of a plant or on a fence. They also hide inside rolled leaves, under loose bark, and under stones or boards. Broad-faced sac spiders wander around at night to find food.

HOW TO SPOT

Size: 0.2 to 0.4 inches (5 to 10 mm) long

North American Range: Southeastern Canada and central and eastern United States

Habitat: Deciduous forests

Diet: Nocturnal insects and dead spiders and insects

SLENDER CRAB SPIDER

(TIBELLUS OBLONGUS)

The slender crab spider has a long body. It can be light brown or pale yellow. A wide, brown stripe runs down the middle of its body. These spiders cling to grass, stems, or leaves. They sit with their legs stretched out in front and behind. This makes them difficult to see. Slender crab spiders are ambush hunters. When prey comes close, the spider quickly runs after it. Female spiders attach egg sacs to thick blades of grass.

HOW TO SPOT

Size: 0.25 to 0.4 inches (6.4 to 10 mm) long

North American Range: Throughout North America

Habitat: Low vegetation, bushes, and tall grasses in lawns, meadows, fields, and marshes

Diet: Small insects including aphids and leafhoppers

TURF RUNNING SPIDER

(PHILODROMUS CESPITUM)

The turf running spider is very flat. Its body is soft and smooth. It can be light brown, gray, or orange. It hunts for prey. The turf running spider often runs in a fast and unpredictable way. It usually chases down prey. Turf running spiders use their silk to make egg sacs.

HOW TO SPOT

Size: 0.16 to 0.24 inches (4 to 6.1 mm) long

North American Range: Canada and northern and western United States

Habitat: Woodlands on the bark and leaves of trees and shrubs, in grasses, and on the ground in leaf litter

Diet: Small insects such as flies

YELLOW SAC SPIDER

(CHEIRACANTHIUM INCLUSUM)

Yellow sac spiders are usually cream to light yellow. They form silk tubes underneath objects or debris on the ground. They can also build silk tubes indoors in the corners of walls and ceilings. The spiders hide in these tubes during the day. Yellow sac spiders may get trapped in sheets, clothing, or shoes. This is when they may bite humans.

FUN FACT

The color of yellow sac spiders can change based on what they eat. For example, if a spider usually eats red-eyed fruit flies, it turns a reddish color. If it eats houseflies, it appears gray.

HOW TO SPOT

Size: 0.16 to 0.4 inches (4 to 10 mm) long

North American Range: Southern Canada and throughout the United States and Mexico

Habitat: Trees, forest floors, shrubs, orchards, and other agricultural areas; buildings and homes

Diet: Insects including leafhoppers and fruit flies

BLACK-TAILED RED SHEETWEAVER *(FLORINDA COCCINEA)*

The black-tailed red sheetweaver is bright red. It is sometimes called the red grass spider. It has a black bump at the end of its abdomen. This spider builds a sheet-like web in the grass close to the ground. The web is about 4 inches (10 cm) across. It has a tangle of silk strands above it. Insects fly into the tangle, which knocks them into the sheet below. The spider then attacks the prey.

FUN FACT

Sometimes a male black-tailed red sheetweaver can be seen on the same web as a female. Both males and females help make webs and clean them.

HOW TO SPOT

Size: 0.12 to 0.14 inches (3 to 3.5 mm) long

North American Range: Southeastern United States

Habitat: Lawns and grassy areas

Diet: Flying insects

BOWL AND DOILY SPIDER

(FRONTINELLA PYRAMITELA)

Bowl and doily spiders are some of the most common spiders in North America. They build their webs between twigs. Each web looks like a bowl on top of a doily or saucer. The spider hangs upside down on the bottom of the bowl. It waits for an insect to fly into the silk threads above the bowl. The insect falls into the bowl. The spider then carries the insect to the doily to eat it.

FUN FACT

Bowl and doily spiderlings move to new places by ballooning. They release a silk thread that catches the wind. Then they float to a new home.

HOW TO SPOT

Size: 0.12 to 0.16 inches (3 to 4 mm) long

North American Range: Throughout North America

Habitat: Bogs, woodland edges, shrubs, and tall grasses

Diet: Flying insects

Web

FILMY DOME SPIDER

(NERIENE RADIATA)

The filmy dome spider has a black or brown abdomen with white stripes. Its web looks like an upside-down bowl or dome. The spider also spins a tangle of lines above the dome. Flying insects hit these lines and fall on the dome. The spider waits on the underside of the dome. When an insect lands on the web, the spider pulls the insect through to the other side and ties it up with silk.

HOW TO SPOT

Size: 0.13 to 0.26 inches (3.4 to 6.5 mm) long

North American Range: Throughout North America, especially in the east

Habitat: Woodlands and woodland edges; in dense, low vegetation; and around houses

Diet: Small flying insects such as mosquitoes and gnats

Web

HAMMOCK SPIDER

(PITYOHYPHANTES COSTATUS)

Hammock spiders are light in color. They have either a stripe or arrow-shaped markings down the back. They construct their webs on buildings, fences, branches, and other plant parts. This spider's web is a sheet that looks like a hammock. Above the sheet is a small maze of strands. The spider can also build a silk retreat or use a leaf to hide. It sits and waits for prey to fall into the web.

HOW TO SPOT

Size: 0.18 to 0.28 inches (4.5 to 7 mm) long

North American Range: Eastern and central Canada and United States

Habitat: Wooded and open areas

Diet: Small insects

CURLYHAIR TARANTULA

(TLILTOCATL ALBOPILOSUS)

The curlyhair tarantula has a dark brown to dark blue body. It has dense, short, dark hairs with some longer golden hairs. The hairs make the spider appear to be a shiny golden-brown color. Like other tarantulas, the curlyhair tarantula lives in a burrow in the ground. It is an ambush hunter. These spiders mate at any time of the year.

HOW TO SPOT

Size: Average 2.4 to 3.6 inches (61 to 91 mm) long

North American Range: Honduras to Costa Rica

Habitat: Tropical areas including rainforests and scrublands

Diet: Insects and small vertebrates

DESERT BLONDE TARANTULA

(APHONOPELMA CHALCODES)

Desert blonde tarantulas are light tan. The male has dark brown or black legs. He also has a reddish abdomen. These spiders hide in burrows during the day. Sometimes they dig their own burrows. Other times, they use old rodent burrows. They can live in the same burrow for many years. They hunt for prey at night.

HOW TO SPOT

Size: 1.9 to 2.7 inches (49 to 68 mm) long

North American Range: Southwestern United States, especially southern California, Arizona, and New Mexico

Habitat: Desert soil

Diet: Lizards, crickets, beetles, grasshoppers, cicadas, and caterpillars

DESERT TARANTULA

(APHONOPELMA IODIUS)

The desert tarantula is covered with pale hairs. Males are darker than females. These spiders live in underground burrows. They line their burrows with silk. The burrows protect the spiders from extreme desert temperatures. Males are ready to mate when they are about ten years old. They search for mates in the fall. After mating season ends, the male soon dies. The females can live to about 25 years old.

Eyes

HOW TO SPOT

Size: 2 to 4 inches (51 to 102 mm) long

North American Range: California, Nevada, and Utah

Habitat: Hot, dry areas

Diet: Insects and small lizards

JOHNNY CASH TARANTULA

(APHONOPELMA JOHNNYCASHI)

The Johnny Cash tarantula was discovered in 2016. The females are brown and black. The males are usually solid black. These spiders breed during the fall. Like other tarantulas, they have large fangs with venom. But their venom is not dangerous to humans. They may bite if they feel threatened. However, Johnny Cash tarantulas are usually very calm. They rarely bite.

HOW TO SPOT

Size: Average 6 inches (152 mm) long

North American Range: The western Sierra Nevada foothills in California

Habitat: Grassy hillsides and deserts

Diet: Insects and other small animals such as frogs, toads, and mice

Female

FUN FACT

The Johnny Cash tarantula was named in honor of the singer Johnny Cash, who sang a song called "Folsom Prison Blues." The spider was first discovered near Folsom Prison in California.

Male

MEXICAN PINK TARANTULA

(BRACHYPELMA KLAASI)

The Mexican pink tarantula is black with pinkish-orange hairs on its legs and abdomen. These spiders make burrows in thorny thickets, rotting trees and stumps, and tall grasses. Mexican pink tarantulas often ambush or hunt for prey close to their burrows. The female makes a single egg sac containing 400 to 800 eggs in her burrow. She guards the egg sac for two to three months until the spiderlings leave.

HOW TO SPOT

Size: 2 to 3 inches (50 to 75 mm) long

North American Range: Mexico's southern Pacific coast

Habitat: Tropical and subtropical dry forests with sandy soil

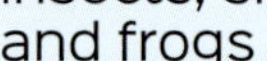

Diet: Spiders, ground-dwelling insects, small lizards, and frogs

MEXICAN RED RUMP TARANTULA *(TLILTOCATL VAGANS)*

Mexican red rump tarantulas are black with long reddish-brown hairs on the abdomen. Females also have reddish-brown hairs on their legs. These spiders dig burrows underground. The burrows can have several chambers. Males die soon after mating. The females make large egg sacs. The egg sacs can contain up to 300 eggs. The spiderlings stay with the female for several weeks. Then they leave to dig their own burrows.

HOW TO SPOT

Size: Up to 3 inches (75 mm) long

North American Range: Florida and parts of southern and southeastern Mexico into parts of Central America

Habitat: Scrublands

Diet: Insects, frogs, mice, and other spiders

MEXICAN REDKNEE TARANTULA *(BRACHYPELMA SMITHI)*

The Mexican redknee tarantula has a black abdomen covered in brown hairs. It is named for the orangish-red spots on the joints of its legs. This tarantula builds a burrow under thorny plants such as cacti. A web carpet extends from the opening of the burrow. At night, the spider waits in its burrow for prey to pass by. It feels vibrations from the prey on the carpet. Then it rushes out and grabs the prey.

FUN FACT

Mexican redknee tarantulas have been featured in movies and TV shows. This is because of their bright colors and calm nature.

HOW TO SPOT

Size: 5 to 5.5 inches (127 to 140 mm) long

North American Range: Mexico's Pacific coast

Habitat: Tropical forests and dry areas with little vegetation such as scrublands, deserts, and dry forests

Diet: Frogs, lizards, mice, and large insects

TEXAS BROWN TARANTULA

(APHONOPELMA HENTZI)

The Texas brown tarantula is dark brown with a light brown cephalothorax. These spiders dig burrows in dry soil. They use their fangs and front legs to move the dirt. The tarantulas sometimes add silk to strengthen the burrow walls. These spiders spend most of their time in the safety of their burrows. During mating season, males leave in search of females. Females attach their egg cases to the walls of their burrows. They guard the eggs until they hatch.

HOW TO SPOT

Size: 3 to 4 inches (76 to 102 mm) long

North American Range: Southwestern United States

Habitat: Grasslands, scrublands, and desert regions

Diet: Insects and other small invertebrates

FUN FACT

To defend themselves, tarantulas can release barbed hairs from their abdomens. These are called urticating hairs. They can irritate a predator's skin and eyes.

CALIFORNIA TRAPDOOR SPIDER *(BOTHRIOCYRTUM CALIFORNICUM)*

The California trapdoor spider is yellowish brown to black. It has shiny legs and some hair on its abdomen. This spider builds a tube-like burrow lined with silk. The spider makes a door at the top that fits tightly into the opening. The California trapdoor spider hides behind the door. It waits until it senses vibrations through the silk. Then it quickly opens the door and grabs the prey, taking it into the tunnel.

HOW TO SPOT

Size: 0.6 to 1.3 inches (15 to 33 mm) long

North American Range: Southwestern United States

Habitat: Dry, sunny slopes

Diet: Insects, frogs, mice, baby birds, baby snakes, and small fish

SUPER STRENGTH

The California trapdoor spider is one of the world's strongest spiders. When under attack, it uses its jaws to hold the lid to its burrow closed. Then it braces its legs against the tunnel wall. The spider has been able to resist a force 38 times its own weight.

FOLDING-DOOR SPIDER

(ANTRODIAETUS UNICOLOR)

The folding-door spider is pale yellow to brown. Its burrow is a long tunnel. The spider covers the walls with a mixture of soil and saliva. Then it lines the walls with silk. The silk lining goes out past the entrance. It forms a small rim that works as a door. The spider pulls the two sides of the rim together to close the door. The door is camouflaged with dirt and debris.

HOW TO SPOT

Size: 0.7 to 0.8 inches (17 to 20 mm) long

North American Range: Eastern United States

Habitat: Dense forests

Diet: Ants, beetles, millipedes, and any other animal that they can overpower

BEACH WOLF SPIDER

(ARCTOSA LITTORALIS)

Beach wolf spiders can be blotchy gray, brown, or white. This helps them hide in their sandy habitat. Beach wolf spiders hunt at night. During the day, they often hide under driftwood, bark, or other debris. Some beach wolf spiders build long, vertical burrows. They use their fangs to dig the burrows. Then they line their burrows with silk.

Size: 0.38 to 0.6 inches (9.6 to 15 mm) long

North American Range: Southern Canada and throughout the United States

Habitat: Sandy areas such as dunes and stream banks

Diet: Nocturnal invertebrates such as crickets

BRUSH-LEGGED WOLF SPIDER

(SCHIZOCOSA OCREATA)

Brush-legged wolf spiders are brown. This spider has a light-colored stripe running down the middle of its whole body. The stripe helps the spider blend in with leaf litter. The male's front legs are black with groups of bristle-like hairs. Like other wolf spiders, the males wave their brushy legs as part of their courtship ritual. They can also make sounds by vibrating body parts against a surface.

HOW TO SPOT

Size: 0.23 to 0.4 inches (6 to 10 mm) long

North American Range: Eastern United States

Habitat: Deciduous forests and open fields near woodlands

Diet: Insects and smaller wolf spiders

BURROWING WOLF SPIDER

(GEOLYCOSA MISSOURIENSIS)

The burrowing wolf spider can be tan, brown, or gray. It digs a deep burrow with its powerful jaws. It lines its burrow with silk. The burrowing wolf spider spends most of its life in the burrow. It enlarges the burrow as it grows. After mating, a female makes an egg sac. The mother cares for the spiderlings for a while after they hatch, carrying them into the sun on her back on warm days.

HOW TO SPOT

Size: 0.6 to 0.8 inches (15 to 21 mm) long

North American Range: Saskatchewan to Ontario in Canada south to Texas

Habitat: Dry, open ground with sandy soils

Diet: Insects such as crickets and beetles and other arthropods including other spiders

CAROLINA WOLF SPIDER

(HOGNA CAROLINENSIS)

The Carolina wolf spider is the largest wolf spider in North America. It has a grayish-brown body. The abdomen has a dark stripe in the center. After mating, a female digs a deep burrow. She builds a tower of silk and twigs around the entrance. The female lays her eggs in an egg sac in the burrow. After hatching, the spiderlings stay with their mother until they can hunt on their own.

HOW TO SPOT

Size: 0.7 to 1.4 inches (18 to 35 mm) long

North American Range: Southern Canada and throughout the United States

Habitat: Open areas in fields, meadows, and forests

Diet: Other spiders, birds, reptiles, amphibians, and insects such as beetles, grasshoppers, cockroaches, and wasps

FUN FACT

Wolf spiders get their name from the way they hunt. They chase down their prey like wolves.

DOTTED WOLF SPIDER

(RABIDOSA PUNCTULATA)

The dotted wolf spider is light brown with dark brown stripes. The underside of the abdomen has a pattern of dark spots. These spiders hunt at night. Sometimes they sit and wait for prey to pass by. Then they pounce and grab it with their legs. Males mate with females in the fall. The females make egg sacs in the late winter or spring. The spiderlings emerge about one month later.

Dotted wolf spider eating grasshopper

HOW TO SPOT

Size: 0.4 to 0.7 inches (11 to 17 mm) long

North American Range: Southeastern United States

Habitat: Tall grasses and weeds

Diet: Insects such as grasshoppers and dead insects

FUN FACT

Wolf spiders are often easiest to find at night. A person can shine a flashlight around their habitat. The spiders' eyes reflect the light the same way a cat's eyes do.

Female eating mate

RABID WOLF SPIDER

(RABIDOSA RABIDA)

Rabid wolf spiders get their name from their fast and unpredictable movements. They are tan or light brown with dark stripes. These spiders are usually found in leaf litter, under rocks, and in tall grass. They can also be found in trash. Rabid wolf spiders hunt both at night and during the day. They do not have a permanent home and move often.

HOW TO SPOT

Size: 0.5 to 0.8 inches (13 to 21 mm) long

North American Range: Central and eastern United States

Habitat: Prairies, woodlands, pastures, cotton fields, and other open areas and in buildings

Diet: Other spiders and small insects such as crickets, grasshoppers, and ants

Female carrying spiderlings

THIN-LEGGED WOLF SPIDER

(PARDOSA PAUXILLA)

Thin-legged wolf spiders are slender and have long legs. They are brown or gray with black markings. A light stripe runs down the middle of the body. The legs have short spines. Like all wolf spiders, thin-legged wolf spiders have eight eyes in a special pattern. The two largest eyes face forward. Two more eyes are on top of the head. The other four eyes are much smaller. They form a row in the front.

Female with egg sac

HOW TO SPOT

Size: 0.16 to 0.22 inches (4 to 5.6 mm) long

North American Range: Southeastern United States

Habitat: Near bodies of water including streams, marshes, beaches, and lakes; on gravel roads and lawns; and in wooded areas and fields

Diet: Insects and other arthropods, including other spiders

TIGER WOLF SPIDER

(TIGROSA ASPERSA)

Tiger wolf spiders are large, dark-colored spiders. They have a narrow line of yellow hairs that runs between the eyes. The legs have light-colored bands. The underside of the abdomen is orange with black stripes and spots. This spider gets its name from this pattern. Tiger wolf spiders dig burrows in the soil. These can be under stones or firewood. The spiders come out at night to hunt. Like many wolf spiders, tiger wolf spiders bite if handled roughly or trapped next to the skin.

HOW TO SPOT

Size: 0.6 to 1 inch (16 to 25 mm) long

North American Range: Southern Canada and midwestern and southeastern United States

Habitat: Forests

Diet: Insects and other spiders

Female with spiderlings

HITCHING A RIDE

A female wolf spider carries her egg sac on her spinneret. She takes it with her wherever she goes. Sometimes the egg sac becomes detached or lost. If this happens, the female frantically searches for it and reattaches it. When the spiderlings hatch, they ride on her abdomen. They stay there until they are ready to leave.

COMMON PIRATE SPIDER

(MIMETUS PURITANUS)

The common pirate spider is white to pale orange. The abdomen is covered by brown, black, and orange markings. This spider has spines on its first two pairs of legs. The common pirate spider takes over the webs of other spiders. First, it plucks on a web's silk lines so the web vibrates. The other spider comes to see if there is prey or a mate. Then the pirate spider kills and eats the other spider.

HOW TO SPOT

Size: 0.16 to 0.2 inches (4 to 5 mm) long

North American Range: Midwestern and eastern United States

Habitat: Dry areas

Diet: Insects and other spiders, especially cobweb spiders, orb weavers, and meshweavers

Egg sac

GARDEN GHOST SPIDER

(HIBANA GRACILIS)

The garden ghost spider is yellow or light brown. The abdomen has small dark markings. Ghost spiders get their name from their pale appearance. They come out after dark to hunt on leaves and other foliage. They spin silk retreats in sheltered places. This can be under a stone or behind some bark. A retreat can also be in a rolled-up or folded leaf. This spider is sometimes found in homes.

HOW TO SPOT

Size: 0.22 to 0.28 inches (5.7 to 7 mm) long

North American Range: Ontario and Quebec in Canada, the United States east of the Great Plains, and Mexico

Habitat: Trees, shrubs, and low foliage

Diet: Small insects

GIANT CRAB SPIDER

(OLIOS GIGANTEUS)

The giant crab spider has a flat tan, brown, or gray body. Like crabs, they can move sideways quickly. These spiders can climb smooth surfaces. In homes, they are often seen high up on walls or ceilings. At night, the giant crab spider hunts. It chases down its prey to capture it. Females guard their egg sacs and spiderlings for about a month.

HOW TO SPOT

Size: 0.4 to 1.9 inches (11 to 48 mm) long

North American Range: Southwestern United States and northern Mexico

Habitat: Dry areas under rocks and shrubs and inside buildings

Diet: Crickets and other arthropods

HUNTSMAN SPIDER

(HETEROPODA VENATORIA)

The huntsman spider has a brown body with spotted legs. Males have a dark pattern on the cephalothorax. Huntsman spiders chase their prey. They capture it with their strong jaws. These spiders have flat bodies. This allows them to fit into small cracks. Females make disc-shaped egg sacs. Each sac holds about 200 eggs. The female carries the egg sac until the spiderlings hatch.

FUN FACT
Huntsman spiders are also called banana spiders. They are often found in shipments of bananas.

HOW TO SPOT

Size: 0.9 to 1.1 inches (22 to 28 mm) long

North American Range: California, Texas, South Carolina, Georgia, and Florida

Habitat: In houses, barns, and sheds; under boards on the ground and other sheltered areas; and in avocado groves

Diet: Cockroaches and other insects found inside homes

OGRE-FACED SPIDER

(DEINOPIS SPINOSA)

The ogre-faced spider has a long, thin, brown body and legs. It looks like a dead twig. Its front two eyes are very large. They are the largest eyes of any spider. They help the spider spot prey at night. The spider's other eyes are very small. Ogre-faced spiders hang upside down and hold their rectangular webs between their front four legs. They launch their webs onto prey passing by.

HOW TO SPOT

Size: 0.4 to 0.7 inches (10 to 17 mm) long
North American Range: Southeastern United States
Habitat: Oak and pine forests, swamps, and marshes
Diet: Insects including crickets, cockroaches, and beetles

SOUTHEASTERN WANDERING SPIDER *(ANAHITA PUNCTULATA)*

The southeastern wandering spider is yellow to light brown. It has a light stripe with a dark outline on the cephalothorax. The spider's legs are long and spiny, and it can curl its legs upward. Southeastern wandering spiders live on plants or in burrows on the ground. They can also be found under rocks or debris during the day. They wander around on the ground to hunt at night. They ambush their prey.

HOW TO SPOT

Size: 0.23 to 0.39 inches (6 to 9.9 mm) long

North American Range: Southeastern United States including Kentucky, Tennessee, Alabama, and Georgia

Habitat: Moist forests and woodlands in warm, humid climates

Diet: Small insects

SOUTHERN HOUSE SPIDER

(KUKULCANIA HIBERNALIS)

The female southern house spider is dark gray or brown. The male is tan with long, thin legs. Only the females spin webs. The female looks for a sheltered crevice to use as a retreat. Then she makes a messy web around it. The strands of the web serve as trip lines. Prey brushes against the strands or becomes trapped in the web. The spider rushes out of its retreat and attacks.

Female, *left*, and male, *right*

HOW TO SPOT

Size: 0.35 to 0.8 inches (9 to 19 mm) long

North American Range: Southern United States

Habitat: Under tree bark and in crevices in houses, barns, bridges, and other human structures

Diet: Insects such as houseflies, horseflies, mud daubers, cockroaches, and June bugs

SPITTING SPIDER

(SCYTODES THORACICA)

Spitting spiders have yellow or orange bodies with black markings. They have six eyes. These spiders hunt mostly at night. But they have poor eyesight. Their front legs are covered with hairs that help them sense the environment. The spider taps its front legs on and around the prey until the prey is between its front legs. Then it spits a sticky, poisonous substance from its fangs that forms a net to pin the prey.

HOW TO SPOT

Size: 0.14 to 0.22 inches (3.5 to 5.5 mm) long

North American Range: Eastern United States

Habitat: Temperate forests and indoors, especially in cellars, cupboards, and closets

Diet: Other spiders, insects such as moths and flies, and arthropods

FUN FACT

It takes only 1/700th of a second for a spitting spider to make a sticky net and capture its prey.

SPRUCE-FIR MOSS SPIDER

(MICROHEXURA MONTIVAGA)

The spruce-fir moss spider is the world's smallest tarantula-like spider. This spider ranges from light brown to a darker reddish brown. In the forests where it lives, mats of moss grow on boulders underneath the trees. These tiny spiders live underneath the moss. The moss provides warmth and food for the spiders. The spiders build tube-shaped webs between the moss mats and rock surfaces.

HOW TO SPOT

Size: 0.1 to 0.15 inches (2.5 to 3.8 mm) long

North American Range: Southern Appalachian Mountains in Virginia, Tennessee, and North Carolina

Habitat: Forests with red spruce and Fraser fir trees at elevations above 5,300 feet (1,615 m)

Diet: Unknown, but likely tiny wingless arthropods called springtails

Spider with egg sac

WOODLOUSE SPIDER

(DYSDERA CROCATA)

The woodlouse spider is native to the Mediterranean area. This spider has a dark orange or red cephalothorax and legs. The abdomen is pinkish or grayish white. The woodlouse spider has six eyes. It has large jaws and two large fangs. This spider hunts at night. The female hangs her egg sac in her silk retreat on the ground. The spiderlings stay with their mother for a few weeks after they hatch.

HOW TO SPOT

Size: 0.35 to 0.6 inches (9 to 15 mm) long

North American Range: Throughout the United States

Habitat: Outdoors in moist areas including gardens, farms, and fields and indoors in basements

Diet: Pill bugs and other arthropods

GLOSSARY

aggressive
Marked by self-assertiveness or a readiness to attack.

ambush
To make a surprise attack from a hidden place.

arthropod
An animal with jointed legs and an exoskeleton.

courtship ritual
A special behavior animals use to attract a mate.

crevice
A narrow crack in a surface.

doily
A small, decorative lace mat.

foliage
Leaves, flowers, and branches.

frond
The large, divided leaf of a palm or fern.

invertebrate
An animal without a spinal column.

iridescence
Having shifting colors based on how the light hits a surface.

leaf litter
Dead leaves and plant material on the ground.

naturalist
A person who studies nature.

retreat
A place to be safe and out of sight.

scrubland
A dry, open area with small bushes and few trees.

spiderling
A young or baby spider.

trip wire
A thin silk thread set by a spider to detect movement or catch prey.

vertebrate
An animal with a spinal column.

TO LEARN MORE

FURTHER READINGS

Mooney, Carla. *Insects and Arachnids*. Abdo, 2022.

Murawski, Darlyne, and Nancy Honovich. *Ultimate Bug-opedia*. National Geographic, 2024.

Whipple, Annette. *Scurry! The Truth about Spiders*. Reycraft, 2022.

ONLINE RESOURCES

To learn more about North American spiders, please visit **abdobooklinks.com** or scan this QR code. These links are routinely monitored and updated to provide the most current information available.

PHOTO CREDITS

Cover Photos: Alex Coan/Shutterstock Images, front (top left yellow bulb); Mark Kostich/Shutterstock Images, front (top right black widow); Shutterstock Images, front (upper left red head, middle left striped, middle left tarantula, middle yellow, middle right, bottom right black and orange); Jamie Spensley/Shutterstock Images, front (upper middle red spines); Sergey Spritnyuk/Shutterstock Images, front (upper right yellow); Malachi Jacobs/Shutterstock Images, front (upper right jumping spider); Tobias Hauke/Shutterstock Images, front (middle brown); Melinda Fawver/Shutterstock Images, front (bottom left); iStockphoto, front (bottom middle red and white); Rav Kark/Shutterstock Images, front (bottom right green); John Dorton/Shutterstock Images, back (left); Danut Vieru/Shutterstock Images, back (right)

Interior Photos: Shutterstock Images, 1 (top left), 1 (top right), 1 (middle), 4 (top), 4 (bottom middle), 4 (bottom right), 6 (top), 8 (top), 8 (bottom), 10 (top), 10 (bottom), 12 (top), 14 (bottom), 16 (top), 21 (bottom), 24 (top), 26 (top), 28 (top), 28 (bottom), 34 (top), 36 (top), 36 (bottom), 37 (bottom), 38 (top), 40 (top), 40 (bottom), 42 (top), 42 (bottom), 43 (left), 43 (right), 44 (top), 45 (top), 46 (top), 47 (top), 47 (bottom), 50 (top), 50 (bottom), 52 (left), 53 (top), 53 (bottom), 54 (right), 55 (top), 56 (top), 56 (bottom), 57 (left), 58 (left), 58 (right), 59 (left), 59 (right), 60 (left), 60 (right), 61 (left), 61 (right), 62 (top), 62 (bottom), 64 (top), 64 (bottom), 65 (top), 65 (bottom), 67 (bottom), 69 (top), 70 (top), 73 (top), 78 (bottom), 80 (top), 80 (bottom), 81 (bottom), 84 (top), 84 (bottom), 86 (top), 86 (bottom), 87 (top), 87 (bottom), 95 (top), 95 (bottom), 101 (top), 101 (bottom), 104 (top), 104 (bottom), 105 (top), 105 (bottom), 107 (top), 107 (bottom), 112 (middle), 112 (right); iStockphoto, 1 (bottom left), 5 (bottom right), 7 (right), 11 (top), 12 (bottom), 16 (bottom), 35 (right), 49 (top), 51 (right), 55 (bottom), 57 (right), 74 (bottom), 82 (top), 82 (bottom), 90 (top), 93 (bottom); Larry Miller/Science Source, 1 (bottom right), 70 (bottom); John Serrao/Science Source, 4 (bottom left), 5 (top right), 14 (top), 17 (top), 23 (left), 24 (bottom), 25 (left), 25 (right), 44 (bottom), 46 (bottom), 48 (bottom), 49 (bottom), 51 (left), 68 (top), 69 (bottom), 72 (top), 72 (bottom), 76 (bottom), 78 (top), 94 (top), 94 (bottom), 96–97, 99 (top), 99 (bottom); Wikimedia Commons, 5 (top left), 11 (bottom), 41 (top), 71 (bottom), 91, 98 (right); Matthew Lindsey/iNaturalist,

5 (top middle), 63 (bottom), 76 (top); Chris A. Hamilton, Brent E. Hendrixson, and Jason E. Bond/ ZooKeys, 5 (bottom left), 83 (top), 83 (bottom); marcophotos/ E+/Getty Images, 6 (bottom), 34 (bottom); Bryan Reynolds/Alamy, 7 (left), 35 (left), 38 (bottom); Ken Schneider, 9; Flickr, 13, 22 (bottom), 27 (bottom), 29 (top), 32 (top), 32 (bottom), 41 (bottom), 52 (right), 66 (left), 66 (right), 71 (top), 89 (top), 89 (bottom), 96, 103; Phil Degginger/ Science Source, 15 (top), 100 (top), 100 (bottom); James H. Robinson/Science Source, 15 (bottom); Stuart Wilson/Science Source, 17 (bottom); Bill Keim/ iNaturalist, 18 (top); Creative Touch Imaging Ltd./NurPhoto/ Getty Images, 18 (bottom); Robert Webster/xpda.com, 19 (top); Clarence Holmes Wildlife/ Alamy, 19 (bottom), 29 (bottom); Ed Reschke/Photodisc/Getty Images, 20 (top), 20 (bottom); Ozgur Kerem Bulur/Science Source, 21 (top); Michael Siluk/ Education Images/Universal Images Group/Getty Images, 22 (top); piemags/Nature/Alamy, 23 (right), 39 (top), 39 (bottom), 79, 102; David J. Green/Alamy, 26 (bottom); Daniel Borzynski/ Alamy, 27 (top); Blanchot Philippe/hemis.fr/Alamy, 30 (top); Stephen Dalton/Science Source, 30 (bottom); Tom Murray, 31, 98 (left); Scott Linstead/Science Source, 33 (top), 33 (bottom), 112 (left); James Carmichael Jr./ NHPA/Photoshot/Newscom, 37 (top); Danny Radius/Science Source, 45 (bottom); McDonald Wildlife Photography Inc./ Corbis/Getty Images, 48 (top); William Donald Fitzpatrick/ Alamy, 54 (left); Ivan Kuzmin/ Science Source, 63 (top); Daniela Duncan/Moment/Getty Images, 67 (top); Jeff Hollenbeck, 68 (bottom); Ozgur Kerem Bulur/ Science Photo Library/Getty Images, 73 (bottom); Avalon/ Universal Images Group/Getty Images, 74 (top); Joseph Berger/ Bugwood.org/University of Georgia, 75 (top); Dan Rieck/ Alamy, 75 (bottom); Addictive Stock Creatives/Alamy, 77 (left); NHPA/Photoshot/Science Source, 77 (right); Rick (RaVen) Hirschl/500px/Getty Images, 81 (top); Frederic Consejo/ imageBROKER/Getty Images, 85 (top); Tony Camacho/Science Source, 85 (bottom); Dr. Paul Zahl/Science Source, 88 (top); A. Cosmos Blank/Science Source, 88 (bottom); Ed Reschke/Stone/ Getty Images, 90 (bottom); Gary Meszaros/Science Source, 92 (top); Rod Planck/Science Source, 92 (bottom); Vstock LLC/ Getty Images, 93 (top); Martin Battilana Photography/Alamy, 97; G. Peeples/USFWS, 106 (top), 106 (bottom left), 106 (bottom right)

ABDOBOOKS.COM
Published by Abdo Reference, a division of ABDO, PO Box 398166, Minneapolis, Minnesota 55439.

Printed in China.
102025
012026

Editor: Marie Pearson
Series Designer: Colleen McLaren
Production Designer: Tara Raymo

LIBRARY OF CONGRESS CONTROL NUMBER: 2025939414
PUBLISHER'S CATALOGING-IN-PUBLICATION DATA
Names: Bell, Samantha S., author.
Title: Spiders / by Samantha S. Bell
Description: Minneapolis, Minnesota: Abdo Reference, 2026 | Series: North American field guides | Includes online resources.
Identifiers: ISBN 9781098298951 (lib. bdg.) | ISBN 9798384932758 (ebook)
Subjects: LCSH: Spiders--Juvenile literature. | Arachnids--Juvenile literature. | Spiders--Behavior--Juvenile literature. | Zoology--Juvenile literature. | Encyclopedias--Juvenile literature.
Classification: DDC 595.44--dc23

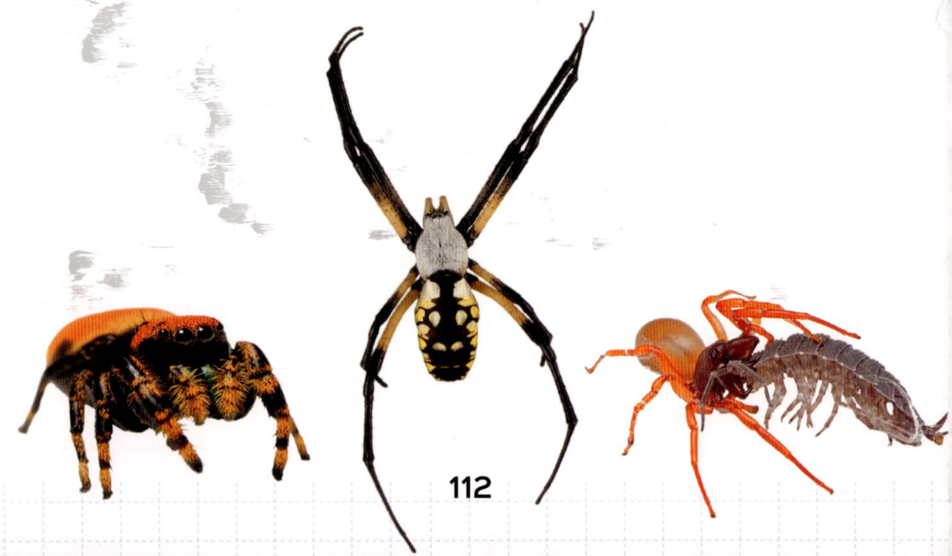